AND THEY ARE COVERED

Amy Acre is a poet, performer and freelance writer from London. Her poem, 'every girl knows' won the 2019 Verve Poetry Prize. Her first pamphlet, *Where We're Going, We Don't Need Roads* (flipped eye) was a Poetry Book Society Pamphlet Choice and a Poetry School Book of 2015.

Amy runs Bad Betty Press with Jake Wild Hall. She co-edited mental health anthology, *The Dizziness of Freedom* (Bad Betty, 2018) and the *Anti-Hate Anthology* (Spoken Word London, 2019). Her work has appeared in *Poetry London*, *Poetry Review*, *Magma*, *3:AM Magazine*, *POEM International: Women on Brexit* and on BBC Radio London.

And They Are Covered in Gold Light

Published by Bad Betty Press in 2019
www.badbettypress.com

Cover design by Amy Acre

Printed and bound in the United Kingdom

A CIP record of this book is available from the British Library.

ISBN: 978-1-9997147-9-6

and they are covered in gold light

PRESS

And They Are Covered in Gold Light

For Jake and Billie

Contents

Your Concerns Are Very Important to Us

on the way to the kitchen i realise i am no longer in my body.
all bodies contain some amount of negative space.
it's ambiguous whether this is you or near you.
on this occasion i pour into the absence, dragging a dead bird,
and the absence receives me like a hostile border force officer.
months later love skirts around the entrance, brandishing an email
confirmation which must be exchanged for a ticket,
skinny jeans gone grey across the knees and bae, i get it.
we are both jealous gods. i too have buckled at empty temples
wondering in which room i would find the 'like a prayer' video.
i remember the covenant, pyrotechnics, everything that falls if you let it
but sweetheart, gravity exists whether or not you believe.
sweetheart, why don't you reach inside yourself to push
your fallen organs back in and tell me if you feel holy.

Mary's Holding Jesus, Not Like a God but Like a Baby, Like I Would Hold My Baby, and They Are Covered in Gold Light.

After David Jones

mary is blue and turquoise
standing on a hill
geisha cheek and charring
mary is rain and dusk
planting a bulb with her lips
bare feet in the moss
kindling
mary is doll white
mary with a lamb
little love
time still before she'll lose him to the world
the gurning jaws of heaven
spread banquet for the men while she waits outside
but they won't know his yawn like a baby owl
smell of yeast and balm
mary blue and brimming
the lamb on her lips
a soft moon
crescent of impossible flesh
mary gold before the trade-off
before he grew infinite
and how she wore it then

stately
metallic
secretly grieving the moon eyes
that would follow her round the room
mary doesn't remember what sex with god felt like
only the sting of something snapped
joseph's breath and beard
three men unwrapping
the infant screech of a goat
mary with thunder that's worse before the coming
like a week late period
mary blue immaculate
blanketed boy on her chest
gone and golden
mary would listen to all his sermons
scan them for in jokes
white smoke
a secret message
anything
but this fucking public man
mary doesn't feel holy stuffing pigskin in bloody knickers
remembers how she bled for weeks after he came
mary full of wine
not the warm waters of galilee
assistant magi
tipsy and trussed up
leotard shine
mary and thirteen men on her right hand

mary with a lamb crackling on a spit
when he blessed her
she wanted to spit in his face
tell him *boy*
i'm the one who wiped away your shit
when the moon came
she sank her teeth in
praying for the sweet bellied child
she tasted wafer dust
her blue mouth powder stuck
dry as an empty church

Hip Hip Hoorah!

After Karel Appel

this is the mother. holder of keys. black ball like a singularity at their centre. full and fingerless. sunbeams radiate from her open mouth and ears the way some people only exist to music.

hear her.

her song is shoulderlift helicopter. her song is bottlenose front crawl. bears and ladybirds attend.

this is a flame raining from the diamond of her crotch. a night she has no door to. it licks the earth like fingers. the taste of soil reminds her of her pregnant body. how full of promise.

this is a sheetoverhead ghost. blueeyed orange little one sitting on yellow's shoulders.
fishtail down. is it halloween already?

this is space where a father isn't. a cat's cradle of night. you lean into the stretch, turn the night sideways like waking to catch a redeye, pluck comet dust from your nails.

this is little old one eye, his spine beside him, butt like a hornet metasoma. bulging. creative. life's work in his liver. blue heart lugging loose. he will be next to go.

this is the family pup in a fuzzy numnah. keeper of the before. black eye punking and full of prank. he sees all, says nothing.

this is the mothersong. sheetoverhead family. a father she has no door to.

this shoulderlift only exists to music. bears raining from the diamond of her redeye. helicopter down. is it sideways already?

this is space that says nothing. it turns the night like fingers. you cradle of liver. you lean into the music.

black eye full of isn't.

this is the

Anecdote

i don't remember unzipping the house
      taking it off my body
      testing my feet
on gravel close enough to hold my unfinished eyes
      i don't remember how far i got
         what the air smelt like
   if i was afraid as the rubix street shifted into secondary
colours
if i stumbled

or if the sudden exit was a million green lights tipping over red
      if my soles found stone with the relief of a returning
lover
slipping their key in the lock
      if the absence of love was love
         my steps
music snapping over paving cracks and
my lips
already rehearsing a brand new story

every girl knows

i was never more than at fifteen . sick and lovely . see the men
jump out the street to check their shadow . see my high rise
skirt , glass tights , double parked eyeliner , apocryphal name ,
smell of monthly embarrassment , suede platforms , scapegoat
thighs , dandruff and blackheads , porn lips , skin lipstick ,
yid nose , cheat bra , cheap heart . men were sick cave puppies ,
new teeth all over catching sun , rumbling like cars . prepping
the school gates or milling asda whistle wolves clawing for
cookies they would read my tshirt . *where you from* and *how old
do you think* and *how about a* fuckage penetrating my lopsided
ego faith of the worst kind . see the men fall out the sky to kiss
rumour . and my best friend was more . unequivocally pretty . i
would stand next to her and liquify , a reflect . she get free
clothes and steak dinner , pocket money , jacuzzi hotel room
with businessman . manga face curve child method actor before
the abortion . worshipping her slaves , a confusion . summer
camp eves were a tally of kisses . ugly me with six but only for
telling . i slutted as a macguffin , closing the narrative of last
year : fourteen . see the man with kind face and chub reading
storybooks to me and brother . see his hand placing under dark
the wax and wane of his fingers . see my atomic . see my
roadkill . see my throb tick sunburn aerobic vomit soft breezing
through the house wave like a giant whale i am in the throat of
crest of all downhill best days of your life enjoy it and stop
crying look it's top of the pops and kat slater . i was never more
than when i was nothing . i was never i never did all shhhh

16

and no . i was a pen from melting . objectivity teething on
gobstopper lust i couldn't give away but i gave it . wet every
day like a spaniel's nose . catching flies on the nightbus , pedalo
lake , tube purgatory , blockbusters , park bench , trocadero ,
mcdonald's , bridge belly , cherry tree , corner shop , rope
swing , climbing frame all ironic joy but only wanted or
worthless , i and the rest colouring ourselves in sticky paint and
promise , chewing chat , boys in their tshirts and genes
bubbling destiny and if love wasn't boy flavour you just
kept quiet love who said anyway who said love no i only . if your
mouth could sing all the animals out of the forest you would ,
wouldn't you . we all method actors pumping puny cocks for
oil waiting for the feelz or feeling daytime soapy drama but
never feeling ourselves . watch out i am so hot i can't even
touch me and days and days of this and not one thing i would
go back for , no not one . did you know if you put enough
posters on your wall you don't need to think , did you know
masturbation is a food group . i am closing on hungry ,
peel my upper lip back baby , see how you roll right in .

Sky Box

you weren't the first man i entered but while the first one
felt like tapping into an unexpected and illegally free channel
on a sky box   getting inside you was more like tapping
on the bones of a bird   breaking them apart until song
filled the room like feathers   after that first time that
in your cafe after closing   your grill-warm chest against the wall
i pushed my fingers under your muscle until you shook
and said no one had made you feel that good   i found
love stuffed into my mouth like feathers i had to fight
not to spit out over your bed because it was too soon

although i had already seen what was inside you
i swallowed the feathers   letting them fly through my body
piling up until   out of deference   my bones hollowed
glass cylinders shot through with light   later
that night in your dirty room   the carpet a velvet sky perforated
with stars made of spliff filters and cat hair   on your bed
that was full of craters   you reached under my wings
to pluck a feather and i rose   levitating   sky
beneath my skin   and looked down on the pinprick
where the earth had been

The Happy Princesses

chiomara carried
her rapist's head
in the dust of her dress
let it rest in her lap
its atlas shatter
let its rust rorschach
galatian hemp and laid
it at husband's feet
so he could unkiss
her mottled mouth
from dead lips

salome for music
and a mother's love
turned heads to dust
all vernix veils and
what have we done
history beating
a ruinous clatter of
mallet on drum
like the clatter of blade
on blade when
zhao sold sun and
moon for an army
to write her name
through

lakshmibai
pistol and steed
for a palanquin
who raised fire to
the raj
who died in the dust

elizabeth un-sistered
lost in a tower
whose turrets thrust
in the image
of their father's cock
an arrow-shaped thing
sharp enough to arrest
kindness at the root
split an atlas

little kings
before you shatter
tell me whose idea
you think it was
to cut and crest
women into rubies
wet thorns stemming
every pink gesture
slicing our heels
for a piece of the pie

tell me if you know
that every princess is a spy
split seventeen ways
from sunday
dust-packed
in the belly of a gun
waiting to burst
through the hearts of men
that she must shatter
everything in her path
before she can rest

Square Inch of You

brush of bear on neon sunrise. screed of fur,
baby shoots and upstart filaments. the effect, a
single line. gestalt pelt soft on the eye and softer
to touch. the bulb of your head, smooth as a
diagram. tilt the insulating surface to assemble
lightbox (see figure j). my thumb scrolls the fibres
into a flip book; every frame corners on your
skin. seeing or flash adapting the captured. let me
filter you in crema, juno, love. glowworm spell.
brush of bear, tresses homogenic and numerous.
each strand, a falling tree, dark as winter sky.

When Your Name Is a Knife

when you first meet her
you are looking for something
that fell off you

the unbelievable charity shop jumper
at a rooftop party
in september

you are looking for your beloved
discontinued
eyebrow pencil
a recent utility bill

when you first meet her
you are under a car
checking your oil
you have no time to worry
about gulls or sea life

she is looking for something
too
something to write her
name through
but not all names are ink

sometimes they are chalk
knowing only how
to hold a body that
isn't moving

*

her body is twice the size
of yours

hardwearing vehicle of tits
and ass in a peasant blouse and denim
hotpants
soft bomb of cyanide in champagne

her body is not your usual type

breasts wagging moray eels stomach of
lump crab meat stomach a mushroom
cloud over backrush but her body is a
hush from the arms of teenage mothers

neurolinguistic whisper trained to pull
nameless desire from mouths like a
wobbly tooth
surprise you so it feels inevitable

her body is open
a coconut cracked against the rotten
wood of a dead fishing boat by uncles
who rise early to catch the ripe young
fruit before they turn brown

double agent
she plunges a tiger claw in the cage of
your chest after making your bed
dinner
back arch in holy abandon

she is a tank a general gathering troops
a junkyard sale a forest fire a fruit knife
peeling off your shell a knife in the back
of an uncle lying facedown in a pailful of
red sand a child with a scream halfway to
her mouth

her body is an infinitely ricocheting
reflection of your desire for yourself
wet
amphisbaenic with one face between your
legs
all vessels

she is your drag king male gaze at the
mirror

a selfie stick angled backwards so you can
disappear up your own arsehole like a
man reading his tweets aloud

her body is divergent
wrapping your relative smallness and
heteronormative femininity in a pink
ribbon of all that is good and invisible

no

her body is fearless
reclaiming paradigms
she stares you out

slung over the windowsill middle finger
plugged in between tectonic thighs

she is a painting of a beauty that predates
atkins and unilever

see how she stands between trees
holding an apple

she is the first time you completed a
flatpack or did your taxes

a dawning era of sufficiency as you sit in a
people carrier next to a castilian animator
grappling with the preterite indicative

her body is the easy disposability of the
contactless generation
ephemeral and boundless
a slur of molecules
a hand on the small of your back as you
hesitate on the periphery of a party

the first touch flickering jellyfish in
montage but once you get down to the
bread and butter of her tongue on your
clit
your fingers in a wall of muscle
the effort of learning her
her body is brought to you by the letters
K and S and the number 27
the silver before dawn

you wake without sleeping and find your
bodies slung across the bed and each other
like the hot cross shadow of window bars

you are
in some way
loveable

her body is hers
she rises into it
her eyes are open

      *

colourless pac-man
eats the sky

                you sit in the cheek

watch pastel
slums pale away

                    as if the most
                    dangerous part
                    was the drop

not being alone
with her in a glass
cage

                  another glass face
                cables the other way

you aim
your phone
and shoot

                                        four pink
                        passengers whose mouths
explode under
your lens

                                      smoke rings
                                      eating air

you aim into the
mouth of the cage

                                       shoot her
                                       from behind

hearing your
fake shutter sigh

                                       she smiles
                                  without looking

then the floor
shudders

                                  she curdles at
                              the rattling lines

lifetime of space
between you and
the pines below

                                     their open
                                  mouths gurning
                                        up at you

greenblack incisors
bared and wolfish

                                    groaning she
                                  drops her head
                                     in your lap

you say *i'll*
protect you

                    you both laugh

raised in
untroubled times
it's easy

                  to believe in your
                  own transcendence

you'd be the one
to survive a flood

                you knead her scalp

making arepas or
massaging
a wound

                as morning's blood-
                        blue

rinse sways you
left

                      and right

paint your mouth
to her ear

                  sing the first
                  four lines

of stormy weather

                  the city
          drowns as you rise

      *

she told you
her real name once

you picked up thread
wove it on sentences
to tease the child
from behind her ear
not realising a name
can be a knife

the third time
approaching the beach
between wax palms
their shadows cutting
cracks in the path
the early sun an air-raid siren
she stopped walking

palming your
assumption-white arm
she told you about
the men who used that name

about pouring a game
of hide and seek into
hours that spill
through the body

you knew then
about cuts so deep

you have to plunge
a hand into your own red
wet to dig up splinters

you didn't know to ask
permission before folding
her into your chest
against the chipshop breeze

but she became breeze
she fell through you
allowed herself
to be held by you

the trees'
pointing spear tops
the sharpened serifs
of a ruthless name

four sunsets later she stands
between you and the door
dark happened

while she was making
you turn out your backpack
looking for notes

she holds the knife straight
and unshaken
as an outstretched hand

*

it's small
as she is big but there's
no ignoring

red-handled metal bee
buzzing drone to her queen
the room closes around
like a fist

titchy thing for shucking skin
off stone-hugging drupe

yesterday she used it
to cut pineapple and now look
she blooms

full weight of her island frame
become one of four walls

you've never before met someone
who could make doors disappear

her eyes that drank you dry
they're deader than salt lakes

but metal bee
drilling its song
doesn't know

you are hard
from sitting on river beds
from sorrow

when she told you
she was repeatedly raped
as a child you wept for her

now you'd push her face
into the sand

metal bee
out of your hands
buzzing into corners
wants to unstone you

the thought you might die
hits with none of the imagined
gravitas
the moment small
spineless

your survival instinct
converts rage into fear
and you pull out a fifty

metal bee in her hand
refracts the outside light
and absolutely nothing
flashes before your eyes

Acknowledgements

Thank you to the editors of *Poetry London*, *Tears in the Fence*, *Closed Gates or Open Arms?* (Verve Poetry Press), *Eighteen* (Culture Matters) and *Mai: Feminism & Visual Culture*, where versions of some of these poems have appeared.

I am hugely grateful to Joelle Taylor, who edited this book, for insight, encouragement and inspiration.

Thank you Sasha Dugdale for ekphrasis, Kat François for a conversation at the Southbank, Roddy Lumsden and all the friends and tutors who have inspired and improved my writing.

Jake Wild Hall—thank you for all the things.

Other titles by Bad Betty Press

Lightning Source UK Ltd.
Milton Keynes UK
UKHW012039020719
345426UK00001B/64/P